Now What?

A Journey to Future Career Success

By

Myriam Mun

Independently published

MOMENTUM
—MOVES MOUNTAINS—

October 2024

First Edition

Printed in the United States of America

ISBN: 9798344487496

Independently published

This book is a work of fiction. Names, characters, places, and incidents either are the product of the author's imagination or are used fictitiously. Any resemblance to actual persons, living or dead, events, or locales is entirely coincidental.

For permissions or inquiries, contact:

myriam.c.muniz@gmail.com

Dedication

To my amazing husband, who supported me wholeheartedly when I decided to take this crazy leap of faith and switch career paths.

We have no idea where this journey will lead, but we're in it together, trusting God every step of the way.

Acknowledgments

Thank you to my mentors, Sue Unvarsky and Olivia Eaddy. Your words of encouragement and guidance were invaluable in the creation of this book. Sue, thank you for your many years of support. "It's ok to be a little uncomfortable" is one of my favorite phrases from you. Olivia, we had an instant connection. I love how all of our check-ins turn into a Godversation (yes, I made that up), but it's so us. I appreciate you both so much.

A special thank you to my good friend, Kristin Dishaw, for coming up with the name of my company, Momentum Moves Mountains, for reading every version of this book, and for humoring my endless logo ideas. I'm so grateful for your encouragement, support, and all our lunches at the beach.

And finally, to my daughter Zahra, my editor and best free client—thank you for your feedback and for always being there to help me bring this book to life.

Table of Contents

Now What?

A Journey to Future Career Success

Introduction

Welcome, dear readers. I'm Jamie, a career coach who's spent decades helping people navigate the often winding and unpredictable roads of their professional lives. Throughout my journey, I've had the privilege of meeting many incredible individuals, each with their own unique story. Today, I want to introduce you to someone truly special—Sofia.

Sofia is at a turning point in her life. She's someone who has always played by the rules, climbed the corporate ladder, and done everything "right." But like many of us, she's come to realize that success on paper doesn't always translate to fulfillment in the heart. Sofia is introspective, a bit dramatic, and, most importantly, ready for a change. She's about to embark on a journey to find a career that not only challenges her but also brings her true joy.

What makes Sofia's story particularly intriguing is her willingness to share it with us. She's allowed us a rare glimpse into her innermost thoughts and feelings through her journal. As we peek into the pages of her diary, you'll see Sofia's struggles, triumphs, and everything in between as she navigates this pivotal moment in her life.

I hope that as you follow Sofia's journey, you'll find insights and inspiration that resonate with your own experiences. Perhaps her reflections will spark conversations with your own career coach or prompt you to explore your own professional path in new ways. Sofia's story is a testament to the power of self-discovery and change, and I believe there's something valuable here for everyone.

So, sit back and join me as we follow Sofia on her quest to chase her dreams. Her journey is just beginning, and I have a feeling it's going to be one worth watching.

Chapter 1: The Big Decision

Querido Diario,

Today was no ordinary day. I found myself sitting on that same old park bench—sí, the one with the suspicious stain that looks like a poorly done Rorschach test. As the late afternoon sun cast long shadows over the manicured lawn, I couldn't help but be reminded of how monotonous my life had become. You know, the usual hum of traffic in the distance, the constant reminder of the bustling city, and the office buildings looming like grey behemoths ready to swallow me whole. "There has to be more than this," I sighed, glaring at the towers of routine and monotony.

For years, I've been the poster child for responsibility, reliability, and efficiency. I could practically write the book on how to be a model employee. Promotion after promotion, and yet, here I am, feeling about as fulfilled as a fish in a desert. Why, oh why, didn't anyone warn me that being a diligent worker bee could be so... unfulfilling?

My sanctuary, the park, usually offers me solace, but today, it felt like a scene from a telenovela where the heroine has her grand epiphany. You know the one—the sun is shining just right, the birds are chirping, and everything is sprinkled with a dash of magic. As I watched a group of kids playing in the distance, their laughter carried by the breeze, it hit me. "Why can't I find a career that makes me as happy as those kids?" I mused, a bit dramatically, I'll admit.

Fast forward to another soul-sucking day at work. There I was, staring at my computer screen, feeling like a caffeinated zombie, when I decided, "Enough is enough!" Yes, diario, I am going to find a career I love. Cue the dramatic music and slow-motion montage of me researching careers, networking, and possibly getting laughed at by a few career coaches.

This decision wasn't easy. It's like stepping off a cliff into the great unknown, where instead of free-falling, you hope to find a trampoline at the bottom to bounce you to success. But for the first time in years, I felt a spark—no, un fuego—of hope and excitement about the future. Bring on the challenges, bring on the failures, because I am ready to find a career that makes me as giddy as a kid on a sugar high.

So, diario, lesson learned: It's never too late to start over. Embrace the decision to find a fulfilling career, no matter how terrifying it might seem. Sofia's saga is just beginning! And who knows? Maybe someday, I'll look back and laugh at how dramatic I was. But for now, I'm off to chase my dreams, one quirky decision at a time.

Until next time,

Sofia's Lesson Learned:

It's never too late to start over. The real challenge is summoning the courage to make the leap. Sure, it's terrifying, but even more frightening is staying stuck in a life that doesn't light you up.

Now What? Next Steps for You

1. **Seek Professional Guidance:** Consider working with a career coach or mentor who can provide personalized advice and support. They can help you navigate the transition and make informed decisions.
2. **Embrace Self-Reflection:** Like Sofia, take a moment to sit in your favorite spot and reflect on what truly makes you happy. Ask yourself, "What would make me feel as joyful as those kids playing in the park?" Use this insight to guide your career exploration.
3. **Challenge the Status Quo:** If you're feeling unfulfilled, question the routine just as Sofia did. Ask yourself, "Is there more to life than this?" Embrace the discomfort of questioning your current path as a step towards finding something more satisfying.

4. **Visualize Your Ideal Career:** Imagine what a fulfilling career looks like for you. Picture the day-to-day aspects and the impact it would have on your happiness. This vision can help you set specific, actionable goals and stay motivated during your job search.

5. **Take Bold Steps:** Following Sofia's lead, don't be afraid to make a decisive move. Whether it's quitting a job you're unhappy with or diving into a new field, take a bold step toward change. This could be starting a new project, applying for a new position, or furthering your education.

6. **Stay Positive During the Transition:** Career changes can be challenging. Embrace the journey with a positive attitude, just as Sofia decided to find joy and excitement despite the difficulties. Stay optimistic and resilient, and be kind to yourself throughout the process.

7. **Keep a Journal:** Like Sofia's diary entries, keep a journal to document your thoughts, progress, and reflections. This can help you track your growth, stay focused on your goals, and maintain motivation as you navigate your career change.

Chapter 2: Building Your Personal Brand

Querido Diario,

Ay, ¡qué emoción! I'm so excited! Today marked the beginning of my grand career transformación, and let me tell you—it was quite the ride! Picture this: Sofia, the once-diligent yet unfulfilled office worker, now embarking on a quest to become... drumroll, por favor... a project manager in the tech industry! Yes, I know it sounds like the plot of a nerdy telenovela, but I promise there's substance to this new chapter.

Enter Jamie, my extraordinary career coach. Think of her as Yoda, but with a far superior wardrobe and advice that's less cryptic. Today's lesson? Building my personal brand. And, oh boy, was it a rollercoaster of self-discovery. Imagine me, Sofia, transforming from a behind-the-scenes worker bee into a notable name in the tech world. It feels like I'm finally stepping into the spotlight.

First things first: self-assessment. Jamie sat me down with one of her signature smiles and asked, "What makes you unique?" I could feel the gears turning in my mind as I reflected on the traits that make me, *me*. It turns out, my love for technology paired with my organizational skills was the secret sauce I hadn't fully appreciated before. Who knew?

Next, Jamie introduced me to personal branding. "Think of yourself as a product," she said. "What's your unique selling point?" Cue the mental montage of me, Sofia, scribbling notes as we defined my brand message: who I am, what I do, and why it matters. It felt like I was writing the script for a blockbuster movie where I'm the heroine, naturally.

The fun part? Building my online presence. Jamie advised me to revamp my LinkedIn profile—professional photo, compelling summary, and a showcase of accomplishments. My profile went from dull and generic to brilliant, as if I'd added a sparkle filter to my career journey. (Okay, no actual glitter involved, but it felt like it.)

Of course, no transformation comes without its challenges. I had moments of self-doubt, imposter syndrome on high, the kind that makes you want to hide under a blanket. But each small step forward felt like a victory. My confidence grew as I realized that building a personal brand is more than just a one-time task. It's an ongoing process of staying true to yourself, evolving, and forming connections that matter.

And guess what? My brand is shining brighter than ever.

Until next time,

Sofía

Sofia's Lesson Learned:

Embrace the power of personal branding. It's about showcasing your unique strengths and passions, building a strong online presence, and continuously learning

and connecting with others. With determination and a bit of sparkle, you can transform your career and make a lasting impact.

Now What? Next Steps for You

1. **Continued Guidance:** Meet with your career coach who will help you shape your brand and guide your career journey.
2. **Identify Your Strengths:** Like Sofia, take time to reflect on what makes you unique. Think about your skills, passions, and what you love to do.
3. **Craft Your Brand Message:** Write a clear, authentic statement about who you are, what you do, and why it matters. Use this as the foundation of your personal brand.
4. **Update Your Online Presence:** Make sure your LinkedIn or website reflects your personal brand. Use a strong, professional photo and highlight your accomplishments.
5. **Stay Consistent:** Building your brand is an ongoing process. Keep refining it as you grow and share your knowledge and experience with others.
6. **Celebrate Your Progress:** Each step, from a LinkedIn update to a new connection, is progress. Acknowledge your growth and stay motivated!

Chapter 3:
Setting Goals:
The Blueprint

Querido Diario,

Oh, the drama! The excitement! Today, Jamie introduced me to the world of SMART goals—Specific, Measurable, Achievable, Relevant, and Time-bound. This framework quickly became my new gospel.

Her first question was a revelation. "Let's start with your ultimate goal," Jamie said, her eyes sparkling with mentor-like wisdom. "What do you really want to achieve? Say it out loud and let's write it down."

I took a deep breath, channeling my inner protagonista. "I want to become a project manager in the tech industry," I declared, surprising myself with the confidence in my voice.

"That's a great goal," Jamie replied, and I swear, I could almost hear a triumphant soundtrack playing in the background. "Now let's break it down using the SMART framework."

And just like that, the blueprint for my future was born:

- Specific: "I want to become a project manager in the tech industry."
- Measurable: "I will complete a project management certification within six months."
- Achievable: "I have the resources and time to study for this certification."
- Relevant: "This aligns with my pasión for technology and organization."
- Time-bound: "I will achieve this by December 31st."

With this clear plan in place, I felt a surge of motivation. Suddenly, my dream didn't seem like some far-off fantasy. It was a structured, attainable goal. Jamie suggested I start by enrolling in a project management certification course. After some intense research (and a few cups of café), I found the perfect program. It covered everything from project planning to team leadership and offered flexible online classes. Perfect for someone like me, juggling a draining job and a budding career change.

You should have seen me, Diario. I set aside specific hours each day for coursework, sticking religiously to my study schedule. I broke down the curriculum into manageable chunks and celebrated each small milestone—yes, there may have been confetti involved.

Jamie was my cheerleader throughout, offering support and sage advice. We met regularly to discuss my progress, work through challenges, and celebrate my wins. She even introduced me to an experienced project manager who shared valuable insights from his own career path.

But let's be real—the biggest challenge was staying disciplined and motivated. There were days when the coursework felt like climbing Mount Everest in heels. My old job drained me, and Netflix always beckoned. But whenever my resolve wavered, I revisited my SMART goals. They were like my personal pep squad, reminding me why I started this journey.

And they worked. "I'm going to do this. I'm going to achieve my goal." These SMART goals are keeping me on track, pushing me closer to success.

Hasta la próxima,

Sofia

Sofia's Lesson Learned: Embrace the Power of SMART Goals.
SMART goals turn dreams into plans, and plans into achievements.

Now What? Next Steps for You:

1. **Define Your Ultimate Goal**
   Take a moment to reflect and write down what you want to achieve. Be clear and specific—what is your big career aspiration?
2. **Use the SMART Framework**
   Break your goal into a SMART plan:
   - Specific: What exactly do you want to achieve?
   - Measurable: How will you know when you've achieved it?
   - Achievable: Do you have the resources or skills to reach this goal?
   - Relevant: How does this align with your passions or long-term vision?
   - Time-bound: What is your deadline for reaching this goal?
3. **Find a Program or Resource**
   Just like Sofia researched her project

management course, take time to find the right program, certification, or training that will help you reach your goal.

4. **Create a Study or Action Plan**
   Set aside dedicated time each day or week to work on your goal. Break the work into smaller, manageable tasks, and commit to a schedule.

5. **Stay Accountable**
   Schedule regular check-ins with your career coach to discuss your progress and any challenges.

Chapter 4: Networking: Building Bridges

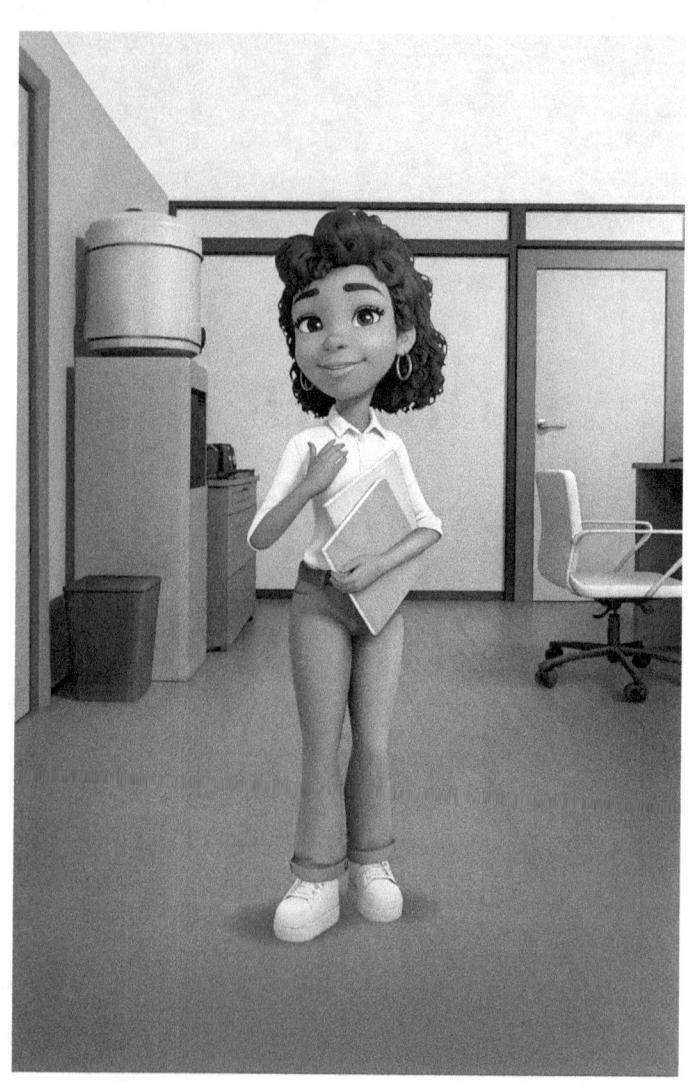

Querido Diario,

Fast forward to the final stretch—drumroll please—by December 31st, I had completed my project management certification! Cue the fireworks, the marching band, and maybe a parade in my honor. Not only did I gain knowledge, but also a newfound confidence in my abilities.

So, here I am, certified and ready to take the next step. This chapter of my journey has taught me the invaluable lesson of using SMART goals to set a clear and attainable path. With determination, focus, and the right support, it's never too late to pursue a fulfilling career.

Hold on to your hat, Diario, because Sofia is about to dive into the treacherous waters of networking! With Jamie's encouragement, I knew it was a crucial step in my journey to becoming a project manager in the tech industry. Feeling confident after meeting Jamie's project manager friend, the first thing I did was attend a local tech meetup.

Picture this: a trendy coffee shop buzzing with tech talk and the aroma of freshly brewed coffee. Armed with a latte and a pocketful of optimism, I stepped into this informal gathering of professionals from various tech backgrounds. I introduced myself to a group deep in discussion about the latest project management software.

"Hi, I'm Sofia. I'm an aspiring project manager, and I recently completed my certification."

The group turned to me, pausing for a moment. Then, one of them, a guy with thick glasses and a T-shirt that read *"I Void Warranties,"* said, "Welcome to the club! I'm Max. We're just debating which project management tool is the least likely to drive us insane."

I smiled. "Sounds like a crucial topic. Mind if I join in?"

At the meetup, I met a variety of people, each with unique experiences and insights. I listened, asked questions, and shared my story and aspirations. Many offered advice and even introductions to others who could help me along my career path. I left feeling more confident and motivated.

Buoyed by my success, I expanded my networking efforts. I turned to LinkedIn, sprucing up my profile to scream "aspiring project manager with a passion for tech and organization." Then, I started sending out personalized connection requests like a modern-day Cupid of the professional world.

My go-to message went something like this: "Hi [Name], I'm Sofia, an aspiring project manager with a passion for technology and organization. I recently completed my project management certification and am eager to connect with professionals in the tech industry. I would love to learn more about your career journey and any advice you might have for someone starting out. Looking forward to connecting!"

To my delight, many responded positively! Some offered virtual coffee chats, others invited me to join online communities, and suddenly, my professional network blossomed. LinkedIn became a treasure trove of information and support, filled with like-minded professionals eager to share their experiences.

Of course, no networking journey would be complete without attending industry conferences and seminars. Picture me, notebook in hand, soaking up wisdom from the gurus of project management. At one conference, I attended a workshop on the future of project management in tech. Not only did I leave with ideas, but I also met several project managers who generously shared tips.

One of the biggest breakthroughs came when a connection from a conference referred me to a project management position at a leading tech company. Yes, Diario, a real job opportunity, all thanks to the power of networking!

And now, without further ado, here are some of my top networking tips:

Sofia's Networking Tips:

1. Attend Industry Conferences and Meetups, these are gold mines for making connections. Engage actively, ask questions, and most importantly, follow up.
2. Use LinkedIn to Connect with Professionals. Keep your profile updated, join relevant groups, and send personalized messages. Engage with content to increase visibility.
3. Join Online Communities Related to Your Field.
   Participate in discussions, ask questions, and share knowledge. These communities provide support, advice, and job leads.
4. Always Follow Up with New Contacts.
   Send a follow-up message after meeting someone new. Express appreciation and reinforce the connection. Keep in touch and offer help when you can.

Networking, I've learned, is about building relationships. Be genuine, interested, and proactive. Each interaction brought me closer to my goal, not just by advancing my career but by learning, growing, and helping others along the way. With each new connection, I built bridges to my future, one relationship at a time.

Hasta la próxima,

Sofia

Sofia's Lesson learned: Networking is about building relationships. Be genuine, be interested, and be proactive.

Now What? Next Steps for You:

1. **Research Meetups or Conferences in Your Field**
   Find a local or online meetup related to your career interests. Commit to attending at least one event this month.

2. **Update Your LinkedIn Profile**
   Make sure your profile highlights your skills, recent achievements, and career goals. Send out personalized connection requests to professionals in your field.

3. **Craft a Networking Message**
   Write a simple message to introduce yourself to new connections. Make it personal and clear about what you're seeking, such as advice or a coffee chat.

4. **Join an Online Professional Community**
   Search for relevant forums or groups in your industry and become an active participant.

5. **Follow Up with New Connections**
   After every networking event or interaction, send a follow-up message to solidify the connection. Offer help where possible and express your appreciation.

Chapter 5: Crafting the Perfect Resume

Querido Diario,

¡Ay, la saga continúa! With my networking game strong, the next beast to conquer was my resume. I knew it had to be more than just a bland list of jobs and duties; it needed to be a showcase of my skills and achievements, something that would make hiring managers swoon. Jamie was there to guide me through the *resume revolution*.

"Your resume is your personal marketing tool," Jamie declared during one of our sessions. "It tells your professional story. You only have one opportunity to make a first impression with recruiters." No pressure, right?

Jamie and I rolled up our sleeves and got down to business. First on the agenda: highlighting transferable skills and tailoring the resume for each application. "Employers want to see how your past experiences have prepared you for the role you're applying for," Jamie emphasized, like a career coach version of Gandalf leading me through the Mines of Moria.

The Great Resume Overhaul Strategy:

1. Focus on Achievements, Not Just Duties

   My old resume was a snooze-fest, listing job duties in the dullest way possible. Jamie taught me the magic of shifting focus from what I did to what I achieved. "Quantify your accomplishments wherever possible," she advised. "Numbers and specific outcomes make your contributions stand out."

   So instead of saying, "Managed office records," I wrote, "Improved office record management system, reducing retrieval time by 30% and increasing efficiency." Boom! Instant wow factor.

2. Use Keywords from Job Descriptions

   Jamie introduced me to the secret of Applicant Tracking Systems (ATS). These systems scan resumes for specific keywords before a human ever sees them. "To get past the ATS, your resume needs to include the keywords used in the job description," Jamie explained.

   I became a keyword ninja, carefully reading job postings and sprinkling relevant terms throughout my resume. If a job description mentioned "project management," "team leadership," and "agile methodologies," you bet those words found their way into my resume (as long as they applied, of course).

3. Keep it Concise and Easy to Read
   "Recruiters spend only a few seconds on each resume," Jamie said. "Make sure yours is easy to skim and doesn't overwhelm them with too much information."
   I streamlined my resume like it was on a Marie Kondo-inspired tidying spree. Unnecessary details? Gone. Bullet points? Check. Clear headings and consistent formatting? Absolutely. I aimed to keep it to one page, focusing on my most relevant and recent experiences.

4. Include a Compelling Summary at the Top
   Jamie recommended starting the resume with a compelling summary that quickly conveys who I am and what I bring to the table. "Your summary should grab their attention and make them want to read more," she said.
   So I crafted this gem:
   "Certified Project Manager in the tech industry. Proven track record of

improving processes, leading successful projects, and increasing team efficiency. Passionate about leveraging technology to drive organizational success."

With my strategy in place, I set to work. I revamped job descriptions to highlight achievements, integrated those crucial keywords, and made sure everything was clear and concise. The summary at the top provided a captivating snapshot of my qualifications.

The transformation was nothing short of miraculous. My resume now looked like it had undergone an extreme makeover. It was professional, clear, and effectively communicated my value. I felt like a proud parent on graduation day as I submitted my resume for various project management positions.

Armed with my shiny new resume, I felt more prepared than ever to tackle the competitive job market and secure the project management role I had been working towards. Here's to the next chapter in the adventures of Sofia, the tech-savvy project manager-in-the-making!

Hasta la próxima,

Sofia

Sofia's Lesson learned:
Your resume is your personal marketing tool. It's your opportunity to sell yourself to potential employers, showcasing your skills, achievements, and suitability for the role. By focusing on achievements, using keywords, keeping the document concise, and including a compelling summary, you can create a resume that stands out and opens doors to new opportunities.

Now What? Next Steps for You:

1. **Review Your Resume for Achievements**
   Replace job duties with specific accomplishments. Where can you add numbers or percentages to show your impact?

2. **Research Keywords for Your Target Role**
   Look at job postings in your field and note the recurring skills or requirements. Make sure your resume includes these keywords.

3. **Streamline and Format**
   Keep your resume concise, ideally one page for early career roles. Use bullet points, clear headings, and consistent formatting for easy readability.

4. **Create a Compelling Summary**
   Write a brief, punchy summary that highlights your key skills, experience, and goals. Make it the first thing recruiters see.

5. **Tailor Your Resume for Each Application**
   Customize your resume for each job by emphasizing the skills and experiences most relevant to that specific role.

OLD RESUME
Sofia Lopez
123 Main Street, Hometown, USA | (555) 555-5555 |
sofia.lopez@email.com

Objective:
I'm looking for a new job where I can work in a good environment and do my best.

Work Experience:
Office Assistant
XYZ Corp | June 2020 – Present
- Answered phones
- Managed files
- Assisted with office tasks
- Worked with different teams
- Handled incoming and outgoing mail

Sales Associate
Big Box Retail | May 2019 – May 2020
- Assisted customers with purchases
- Processed returns and exchanges
- Stocked shelves and maintained inventory
- Operated the cash register
- Worked with team members to meet sales goals

Receptionist
ABC Law Firm | June 2018 – April 2019
- Greeted visitors
- Answered calls and directed them to appropriate departments
- Scheduled meetings for lawyers
- Organized files and documents
- Performed general office duties

Skills:
- Communication
- Time management
- Problem-solving
- Teamwork
- Microsoft Office

Education:
Bachelor's Degree in Communications
State University | Graduated: May 2018

References:
Available upon request

NEW RESUME
Sofia Lopez

123 Main Street, Hometown, USA | (555) 555-5555 |
sofia.lopez@email.com | [LinkedIn Profile Link]

Summary

Certified Project Manager with over three years of experience in the tech industry. Proven track record of leading cross-functional teams, managing successful projects, and improving processes. Passionate about leveraging technology to drive efficiency and deliver projects on time and within scope. Adept at using Agile methodologies and project management software. Seeking to contribute to a dynamic organization by managing and delivering impactful tech projects.

Work Experience

Project Manager (Certification Internship)
XYZ Tech Solutions | March 2023 – August 2023

- Led a team of 10 to implement a new project management software, reducing project turnaround time by 20%
- Coordinated with stakeholders across departments to ensure successful project execution within scope and budget
- Conducted weekly progress meetings, resolving issues that improved team efficiency by 15%
- Managed all project documentation and reporting, utilizing tools like Jira and Trello
- Delivered project two weeks ahead of schedule, receiving commendations for exceptional leadership and management

Office Assistant (Relevant Skills: Project Coordination)
XYZ Corp | June 2020 – Present

- Coordinated office-wide initiatives, including the implementation of a new document management system, improving data retrieval by 30%
- Managed cross-departmental projects such as annual compliance audits, ensuring timely completion
- Developed and maintained timelines for office renovation project, keeping tasks on track and within budget
- Supported teams in planning and executing events, creating detailed project plans and task lists

Sales Associate (Transferable Skills: Customer Management)
Big Box Retail | May 2019 – May 2020

- Provided leadership during peak sales periods, creating and managing schedules to optimize staff productivity
- Introduced a new inventory management process, reducing discrepancies by 15%
- Regularly collaborated with store management to develop sales strategies, resulting in a 10% increase in monthly sales

Skills
- Project Management (Agile, Waterfall)

- Team Leadership and Coordination
- Process Improvement
- Risk Management
- Stakeholder Communication
- Project Management Tools: Jira, Trello, Asana, Microsoft Project
- Microsoft Office Suite (Excel, Word, PowerPoint)
- Fluent in English and Spanish

Certifications
- Certified Associate in Project Management (CAPM) | PMI | 2023
- Google Project Management Professional Certificate | Coursera | 2023

Education
Bachelor of Arts in Communications
State University | Graduated: May 2018

Projects
New Product Launch Project – XYZ Tech Solutions
- Managed the launch of a new SaaS product, leading a cross-functional team from concept to delivery
- Created a detailed project timeline, managed the budget, and delivered the product launch on schedule
- Reduced project risk by implementing a change management process that increased team adaptability by 25%

Professional Associations
- Member, Project Management Institute (PMI)
- Member, Women in Tech Network

References
Available upon request

Chapter 6: Mastering Interview Preparation

Querido Diario,

¡Ay, the saga continues! The next chapter in my career makeover was more nerve-wracking than a reality TV finale. The time came for job interviews—a real test of my mettle. With my freshly minted resume and growing network, the interview invites started rolling in. Each one felt like a mix of a golden ticket to Willy Wonka's factory and a summons to a medieval trial by combat.

"Your resume is your first impression, but interviews are where you show why you're the best fit for the gig," Jamie said, "Being prepared not only boosts your confidence but also shows how much you want it."

Sofia's Interview Prep Routine:

1. **Research the Company and Role Thoroughly**
   Jamie stressed how crucial it was to get the vibe of the company and role. So, I went full detective mode, digging into company histories, missions, and values. I dissected job descriptions like a science project, making notes on the must-have skills and traits. This

sleuthing helped me tailor my answers and show I was a perfect match.

2. **Prepare Answers to Common Interview Questions**

Jamie gave me a list of common questions, and we crafted responses that were solid gold. Think:

- ○ "Tell me about yourself."
- ○ "What are your strengths and weaknesses?"
- ○ "Why do you want to work here?"
- ○ "Describe a tough situation and how you handled it."

I used the STAR method (Situation, Task, Action, Result) to frame my responses. For example, when asked about a challenge, I would say:

- S: "In my last role, we faced a tight deadline for a big project."
- T: "As the lead, I was responsible for hitting the mark without compromising quality."
- A: "I reorganized tasks, set clear milestones, and conducted daily check-ins."

- R: "We delivered the project on time, earning high praise from the client."

3. **Practice with Friends or Mentors**
   Practicing was key to building confidence. I roped in trusted friends for mock interviews, and Jamie threw in curveball questions to keep me on my toes. It was like boot camp for my nerves, helping me polish my delivery and refine my answers.
4. **Dress Sharp and Show Up on Time**
   First impressions matter, Jamie reminded me. "Dress sharp and show respect for the opportunity." I chose outfits that matched each company's vibe, from corporate suits to business casual looks. For virtual interviews, I did tech checks beforehand to avoid any surprises.

The Big Day

On interview day, it felt like I was stepping onstage for a packed crowd. I arrived 15 minutes early, as Jamie suggested, giving myself time to review my notes and breathe.

One last moment in the bathroom to go into Wonder Woman mode (thanks, Amy Cuddy!), and I was ready. When I sat down with the interviewer, I greeted them with a warm smile and a firm handshake (sweaty palms aside).

I answered each question with clarity and confidence, using the STAR method for behavioral questions. When they asked why I wanted the job, I nailed it—talking about their exciting projects and how they aligned with my own passions. Throughout the interview, I made eye contact, asked thoughtful questions, and showed genuine enthusiasm for the company and the role.

The Offer

After a few rounds of interviews, all my hard work paid off. I received a call from the hiring manager, saying, "Sofia, we were really impressed with your interview and your background. We'd love to offer you the project manager role."

Cue the confetti and victory dance! I accepted the offer with gratitude and excitement, eager to start this new chapter of my career.

As I hung up, I couldn't wait to tell Jamie the news. Without her guidance, I might not have had the confidence or the skills to make it this far. The entire process taught me that interviews are no longer a source of anxiety—they're my opportunity to showcase my passion and skills.

Hasta la próxima,

Sofia

Sofia's Lesson Learned: Preparation is Key to Interview Success

Mastering interview preparation teaches that success in interviews hinges on thorough preparation. By researching the company and role, preparing detailed responses to common questions, practicing with others, and ensuring a polished appearance and punctuality, approach each interview with confidence. These steps will not only help you articulate your fit for the role but also showcase your enthusiasm and readiness.

Now What? Next Steps for You:

1. **Research the Company and Role Thoroughly**
   - Look into the company's mission, values, and recent news. Understand the role's responsibilities and required skills.
   - Use this information to tailor your answers and demonstrate why you're a great fit.

2. **Prepare Answers to Common Interview Questions**
   - Practice responses to typical questions like "Tell me about yourself," "What are your strengths and weaknesses?" and "Why do you want to work here?"
   - Use the STAR method to structure your answers for behavioral questions.

3. **Conduct Mock Interviews**
   - Practice with your career coach, friends, family, or mentors. Simulate real interview conditions to build confidence and receive feedback.
   - Prepare for both standard and unexpected questions.

4. Dress Appropriately and Plan Your Arrival

- Choose attire that fits the company's culture and dress code. Plan your route to the interview location or check your tech setup for virtual interviews.
- Aim to arrive or log in a few minutes early to settle in and review your notes.

5. Follow Up

- After the interview, send a thank-you note or email expressing your appreciation for the opportunity and reiterating your enthusiasm for the role.
- Use this chance to briefly restate why you're a great fit and address any key points discussed during the interview.

Chapter 7: The Power of Mentoring

Querido Diario,

I can't forget to talk about the power of mentoring. Life, as you know, loves a good twist. Throughout this journey, I found myself immersed in something even more profound: the magic of mentoring, thanks to the wise Jamie.

Jamie's guidance has been a game-changer. She's my personal Yoda, with advice that actually makes sense and hair that's always on point. Our regular meetings have become my lifeline, filled with advice, encouragement, and insights you couldn't buy for all the lattes in the world.

One evening, we decided to shake things up and ditch our usual coffee spot for a more vibrant place—a local karaoke bar. Jamie, known for her straight talk and surprises, unexpectedly let slip her love for karaoke. And me, a bit nervous but intrigued, watched as Jamie unleashed her inner diva with an enthusiastic rendition of "I Will Survive."

As the night progressed, Jamie nudged me to join her on stage. Despite my initial hesitation, I chose a song and took the mic. Starting off a bit shaky, I soon found my groove, fueled by Jamie's enthusiastic cheers. Our impromptu karaoke duet became a metaphor for our mentoring bond—encouraging each other to break boundaries, embrace challenges, and shine in new experiences.

One afternoon, over our usual caramel macchiatos at our cozy coffee spot, Jamie took me on a trip down memory lane. "I remember my first shot at leading," she started, a nostalgic grin lighting up her face. "It was a disaster. I made so many mistakes. But my mentor didn't scold me. She helped me see where I went wrong and how to do better next time."

As I absorbed her story, it hit me how valuable these pearls of wisdom really were. Jamie's stories weren't just tales; they were roadmaps full of twists, bumps, and U-turns, showing me that even the best stumble before they soar.

Regular Meetings for Advice and Encouragement

Our meetings are like pit stops in a marathon, fueling my motivation and strength. Whenever I hit a bump in the road, Jamie's right there, offering practical solutions and pep talks that could rival any motivational speaker. These sessions keep me laser-focused on my goals and remind me of my potential.

Learning from Jamie's Experiences and Mistakes

Jamie's honesty about her errors has been eye-opening. She taught me that mistakes are just steps in the learning process. What matters is how you respond and what you learn from them. This perspective has changed how I approach challenges, making me see setbacks as opportunities to grow instead of roadblocks.

Sharing Knowledge and Supporting Peers

Inspired by Jamie, I've started sharing my newfound wisdom with my colleagues. Mentoring isn't just about receiving advice; it's about giving back too. I've begun informal mentoring sessions at work, where we swap ideas, offer support, and celebrate our small victories together.

One unforgettable day, my colleague Rachel came to me in a panic, overwhelmed by an upcoming project deadline. Drawing from my Jamie-inspired toolkit, I helped her break down the project into manageable tasks and set realistic deadlines. "Thank you, Sofia," she said, visibly relieved. "Your advice really helped. I don't feel as stressed now."

Her gratitude filled me with a sense of satisfaction I hadn't expected. Mentoring Rachel was rewarding, reinforcing the idea that mentoring is indeed a two-way street. By helping others, I'm also solidifying my own knowledge and skills.

Lesson: Mentoring is a Two-Way Street

Mentoring isn't just about guidance; it's about building a supportive network where both parties learn and grow. My experience with Jamie taught me the importance of having a mentor for ongoing support and advice. But equally, becoming a mentor myself brought immense joy and fulfillment, proving that helping others achieve their goals is just as rewarding as achieving my own.

Mentoring had a profound impact on both my career and personal development. It equipped me with tools to navigate challenges, boosted my confidence to chase my dreams, and gave me the chance to make a real difference in others' lives. The ripple effect of mentoring was clear—knowledge and support shared between two people could extend far beyond, fostering a culture of growth and collaboration.

Looking back on my journey, I felt immense gratitude for Jamie's mentorship. It had been my guiding light, empowering me to reach my full potential. Now, as a mentor myself, I am committed to continuing this tradition, helping others find their way and achieve their dreams.

So, dear diary, here's to the next chapter in this rollercoaster ride of a career. With Jamie's wisdom and my newfound role as a mentor, I'm ready to embrace whatever twists and turns lie ahead.

Hasta la próxima,

Sofia

Sofia's Lessons Learned: Mentoring is a Two-Way Street

Mentoring isn't just about receiving guidance; it's also about giving back. By working with a Career Coach you will see the importance of having a mentor for ongoing support and advice. It can lead to becoming a mentor yourself and see that helping others achieve their goals is just as rewarding as achieving your own.

Mentoring can profoundly impact both your career and personal development. It equips you with tools to navigate challenges, boosts your confidence to chase your dreams, and allows you to make a real difference in others' lives. The ripple effect of mentoring was clear—knowledge and support shared between two people extend far beyond, fostering a culture of growth and collaboration.

Now What? Next Steps For You:

1. **Find a Mentor:**
    - Identify Your Goals and Needs: Determine what specific guidance you're seeking and what qualities you value in a mentor.
    - Look Within Your Network: Reach out to colleagues, supervisors, or industry contacts who have the

experience and qualities you're looking for.

- Attend Industry Events: Engage in networking events, seminars, and workshops to meet potential mentors who are experts in your field.
- Seek Out Professional Organizations: Join relevant professional organizations or groups where you can connect with experienced individuals willing to offer mentorship.
- Be Proactive: Don't hesitate to approach potential mentors with a clear idea of how you could benefit from their guidance and how you can also offer value in return.

2. **Working with a Mentor:**
- Set Clear Goals: Discuss and establish specific goals for the mentoring relationship. Outline what you want to achieve and how you will measure success.
- Schedule Regular Meetings: Arrange regular meetings to ensure consistent progress. Be punctual and respectful of your mentor's time.
- Prepare for Meetings: Come prepared with questions, updates on progress, and topics for discussion. This will make the sessions more productive and focused.

- Be Open to Feedback: Listen actively to your mentor's advice and be willing to act on it. Constructive feedback is essential for growth.
- Show Appreciation: Express gratitude for the mentor's time and guidance. Acknowledge their impact on your development.

3. **Managing Multiple Mentors:**
    - Identify Different Needs: Understand that different mentors may provide guidance in various areas. For example, one mentor might help with career development, while another might focus on specific skills or industry knowledge.
    - Establish Boundaries: Clearly define the roles and expectations for each mentoring relationship. Avoid overlap or conflicts by being transparent about your goals with each mentor.
    - Coordinate Efforts: If working with multiple mentors, ensure that their advice complements rather than contradicts. Communicate with them about your overall progress and any challenges you're facing.

4. **When to End a Mentoring Relationship:**
    - Assess Progress: Regularly evaluate whether the mentoring relationship is helping you achieve your goals. If

you're not making progress or if your needs have changed, it might be time to reconsider the relationship.

- ○ Communicate Clearly: If you decide to end the relationship, do so respectfully. Thank your mentor for their support and explain your reasons honestly.
- ○ Reflect on the Experience: Take time to reflect on what you've learned from the relationship and how it has contributed to your growth. Use these insights to guide your future mentoring relationships.

5. **Expand My Role as a Mentor:**
   - ○ Formalize my mentoring sessions at work by creating a structured program for peer support.
   - ○ Identify additional colleagues who could benefit from guidance and offer to mentor them.

6. **Develop Mentorship Skills:**
   - ○ Seek out resources or training on effective mentoring to enhance my ability to support others.
   - ○ Reflect on my mentoring experiences and gather feedback to continually improve my approach.

7. **Share Mentoring Experiences:**
   - ○ Write a blog post or article about my journey with mentoring, highlighting the benefits and insights gained.

- Present on the value of mentoring at team meetings or industry events to inspire others.

8. Support and Celebrate Peers:
- Continue to offer support and celebrate the achievements of my colleagues.
- Create opportunities for team members to share their successes and learnings.

Chapter 8:
Setting
Financial Goals

Querido Diario,

Let me tell you about my newest adventure: financial planning! With a new job lined up, I realized that professional success wouldn't be complete without setting some solid financial goals. That's when Jamie introduced me to Alex, a certified financial coach who could explain compound interest like it was a bedtime story.

"Meet Alex," Jamie said during one of our café meetings. "He's here to help you create a solid financial plan and guide you through budgeting, saving, and investing."

With Alex's help, I embarked on a crash course in financial literacy. Here's how we built my financial roadmap:

Sofia's Financial Plan:

1. Create a Monthly Budget: Alex started with the basics—budgeting. We listed my expected income and all my monthly expenses, from rent and utilities to my beloved coffee runs. It was an eye-opener to see just how much I was spending on non-essentials like takeout and impulse buys. With Alex's guidance, I set limits and committed to sticking to a budget.
2. Set Aside an Emergency Fund: Alex stressed the importance of having an emergency fund. "Life is unpredictable," he

said, "and you need a financial cushion for unexpected expenses." We calculated how much I would need to save to cover six months of expenses. It felt good to know I'd have a safety net if anything went wrong.

3. Start Investing: Once my budget and emergency fund were in place, Alex introduced me to the basics of investing. He explained how investing helps grow your money through compound interest and emphasized the importance of diversification. I started contributing to a simple mutual fund and planned to consult a financial advisor for a more tailored investment strategy.

4. Plan for Retirement Early: Retirement planning was something I hadn't really thought about, but Alex explained how crucial it is to start early. He walked me through options like 401(k)s and IRAs, and I felt motivated to take advantage of employer-sponsored retirement plans, especially those with matching contributions.

With Jamie and Alex's guidance, I felt empowered to take control of my financial future. I set clear goals, built a budget, started investing, and planned for retirement. These steps didn't just give me peace of mind—they created a foundation for long-term security and independence.

And when life threw me a curveball—like my car breaking down unexpectedly—my emergency fund was there to save the day. I didn't have to stress about how to pay for the repairs, and it was a reminder that financial planning really works.

So, dear diary, here's to building financial wisdom! With Jamie and Alex by my side, I feel ready for whatever life brings.

Hasta la próxima,

Sofia

Sofia's Lessons Learned:

- **Start Early: The sooner you begin planning and saving, the more time your money has to grow.**
- **Stay Disciplined: Stick to your budget and consistently save and invest for long-term stability.**
- **Be Prepared: An emergency fund provides peace of mind when life throws unexpected challenges your way.**

Now What? Next Steps For You:

1. **Create a Budget:**
    - Start by listing your income and monthly expenses.

- Track your spending to identify areas where you can cut back.
- Set a realistic budget and commit to following it.

2. **Build an Emergency Fund:**
   - Aim to save enough to cover 3-6 months of living expenses.
   - Set aside a portion of your income each month into a separate savings account.
   - Use this fund only for true emergencies like medical bills or unexpected repairs.

3. **Start Investing:**
   - Learn about different investment options, such as stocks, bonds, and mutual funds.
   - Consider starting with low-risk, diversified funds.
   - Consult a financial advisor to tailor your investment strategy to your goals and risk tolerance.

4. **Plan for Retirement:**
   - Take advantage of employer-sponsored retirement plans like 401(k)s, especially if there are matching contributions.
   - If possible, open an IRA to supplement your retirement savings.
   - Start contributing early to give your savings time to grow.

5. **Review and Adjust Your Financial Plan Regularly:**
    o   Set time aside every few months to review your budget, savings, and investment progress.
    o   Adjust your plan as your financial situation or goals change.
    o   Stay consistent with saving and investing for long-term stability and growth.

Chapter 9: Embracing the Journey

Querido Diario,

Here we are, at the final chapter of what has been nothing short of a rollercoaster ride. Today, as I sit at my desk, surrounded by the familiar hum of the office and the symphony of clattering keyboards, it's hard to believe it's been two years since I decided to turn my life upside down. My journey has been filled with purpose, ambition, and a lot of coffee.

Looking back, I'm genuinely amazed at how far I've come. I remember those initial steps, filled with more trepidation than a cat meeting a cucumber. But once I had a clear vision of my career goals, I was unstoppable. Late nights became my norm as I enrolled in online courses, mastering new technologies and methodologies that were shaping the industry. My determination was a force to be reckoned with, driven by a vision of the future me, confidently leading projects and inspiring teams.

One of the best decisions I made was finding a career coach. Working with Jamie was the catalyst that turned my dreams into achievable goals. Jamie wasn't just there to tell me what to do—she helped me map out my path, sharpen my skills, and keep my confidence high. With her guidance, I stopped feeling lost and instead took control of my career journey. Having a coach by your side really makes the difference, especially when facing career transitions or challenging decisions.

Building a network was also a game-changer. Industry events, networking meet-ups, and countless LinkedIn connections forged a web of relationships that buoyed me up. My mentors, the real-life Yodas of my journey, shared their wisdom and experiences, guiding me through the labyrinth of my new field. Their support was like a GPS, recalibrating me whenever I veered off course.

Crafting a standout resume was another Herculean task. Every word was chosen with precision, highlighting my strengths and accomplishments. I presented myself as a capable and driven professional, ready to take on the world. And guess what? It worked.

Interviews, once my nemesis, became opportunities to shine. I learned to articulate my value with confidence. I no longer dreaded the question, "Why should we hire you?" Instead, I welcomed it as a chance to show how I could uniquely contribute to any team or project.

Financial goals were also part of my journey. With Alex's sage advice, I navigated the waters of budgeting, saving, and investing. My finances stabilized, and I laid the groundwork for future investments. It was like learning to dance—initially awkward, but with practice, I found my rhythm.

Now, as I look at the stack of projects on my desk and the emails vying for my attention, I feel a deep sense of fulfillment. My career is no longer a series of jobs; it's a purposeful path toward my aspirations. Starting over wasn't just about rebuilding; it was about reaching higher than ever before.

Turning to the window, I see the city skyline bathed in the warm glow of the setting sun. It's a reminder that each day brings new opportunities. Jamie's words echo in my mind: "What you focus on will grow." With a smile, I dive back into my work, knowing that my future is indeed bright.

This isn't just the conclusion of a chapter; it's the beginning of a new phase filled with endless possibilities. My goals are set, my network is strong, my resume is polished, my mentors are guiding me, my interview skills are honed, and my financial plan is solid. I'm ready to face whatever challenges lie ahead.

Hasta la próxima,

Sofia

Sofia's Final Thoughts:

My journey has been a testament to resilience, continuous learning, and the value of supportive relationships. By embracing change, setting clear goals, and staying committed to my personal and professional growth, I've transformed my life and career. Starting over is

never easy, but it's one of the most rewarding things you can do. A career coach like Jamie helps transform uncertainty into clarity, providing direction, accountability, and strategies for long-term success.

Let my story serve as an inspiration to anyone considering a fresh start. With the right mindset, support, and dedication, we can overcome any obstacle and achieve our dreams. Embrace the journey, stay positive, be persistent, and most importantly, enjoy the ride.

Next Steps for Career and Financial Success:

1. **Find a Career Coach:**
   - Working with a career coach helps you clarify your goals, map out a strategy, and stay accountable. Having someone guide you through the tough decisions is invaluable.
2. **Set Clear, Achievable Goals:**
   - Identify where you want to be in your career, set clear milestones, and track your progress consistently. Break big goals into smaller, manageable tasks.
3. **Strengthen Your Network:**
   - Attend industry events, build relationships on LinkedIn, and seek

out mentors. Surround yourself with people who can help you grow and provide fresh perspectives.

4. **Sharpen Your Interview and Resume Skills:**
    - Ensure your resume highlights your strengths and accomplishments. Practice interviews to confidently articulate your value and how you can contribute to the team.

5. **Create and Stick to a Financial Plan:**
    - Establish a budget, build an emergency fund, and start investing for the future. Work with a financial advisor if needed, and ensure your financial goals align with your long-term career plans.

Your career and financial journey is an ongoing process—be proactive, seek help when needed, and always stay focused on your goals.

Bibliography for *Now What? A Journey to Future Career Success*:

Books/Articles:

- Cuddy, A. (2015). *Presence: Bringing Your Boldest Self to Your Biggest Challenges*. Little, Brown and Company.

Websites:

- MindTools. (n.d.). *SMART Goals: How to Make Your Goals Achievable*. https://www.mindtools.com/pages/article/smart-goals.htm
- Indeed Editorial Team. (2021, June 9). *How to Use the STAR Interview Response Technique*. Indeed. https://www.indeed.com/career-advice/interviewing/how-to-use-the-star-interview-response-technique

Myriam Muniz

Born and raised in Spanish Harlem, Myriam has spent the last few years living in Florida with her husband and four dogs. With over 30 years of experience in the Retirement Industry, she has honed her skills as a leader, mentor, and coach, guiding individuals both personally and professionally towards success and growth. Despite being an introvert, Myriam has a unique ability to engage in meaningful conversations and uses her compelling speaking voice to advocate for her faith and her passion for helping others reach their full potential.

As the coordinator of Real Talk with Victor and co-owner of the nonprofit 240 to 3:16 Ministries alongside her husband, Myriam is deeply committed to serving communities through prison ministry and local and global outreach initiatives. Her dedication to making a difference extends beyond the professional realm, as she actively participates in church activities and contributes to various community-driven endeavors.